Home Time

A BOOK TO ENTERTAIN YOUR CHILD

LET'S PRETEND

Written and compiled by Pamela Mainprize and Moira Howes
Illustrated by Diana Bowles and Anne Parsons

Home Time is a series of six books, each designed t~ ~~~ ~ht ideas!
Each chosen item has been tested with c' ~ccess.
You will find fresh ideas, with clear instru~ child
throughout the year, in any weather, u. ~ts.

D1638844

HENDERSON
PUBLISHING PLC
©1995 HENDERSON PUBLISHING PLC

LET'S PRETEND

Page

5   Zoos

6   Farm Layouts

6   Vets

7   Pet Shows

8   Cafés and Restaurants

10   Cops and Robbers

11   Cowboys and Indians

12   Fairies, Princes and Princesses

13   Funfairs

14   Garages

15   Hairdressers

16   Hospitals, Doctors, Dentists

18   Libraries

19   Making Music

20   Mummies/Daddies

21   Offices

22   Play Food

24   Play Money

24   Play Dough Recipe

25   Post Offices

26   Puppet Shows

28   Roadways and Villages

29   Schools

Page

30   Fish and Chip Shop

31   Clothes Shop

31   Grocery Shop and Supermarket

32   Newsagent

32   Shoe Shop

33   Spaceships

34   Sports Day

36   Swimming Pools

37   Tea Parties and Picnics

38   Tents and Dens

39   Top of the Pops

40   Airports

41   Rowing Boat

41   Car Ferry

42   Container Ship

42   Pirate Ship

43   Buses

44   Fire Engines

45   Racing Cars

46   Trains

47   Washing Day

48   Witches, Wizards and Ghosts

GAMES UNLIMITED

*This book contains over 40 play ideas suitable for children aged
3 - 7 years. The ideas are based on imagination and take the form
of role play or 'let's pretend' games.*

*Role play allows children to absorb new information and relate to
the world around them by acting out situations they have experienced.
For example, they may want to play doctors or dentists after a recent
visit, or perhaps at fire engines if they have seen one racing past that day.
Both types of game will stimulate your child's imagination and help to
expand their vocabulary, but above all they are FUN to play.*

*Each idea contains suggestions
for setting up the game. The play
materials listed can usually be
found around the home; others
can be obtained free of charge or
bought at little cost. However,
they are only suggestions to add
to the enjoyment of the game but
they can all be substituted by
imagination!*

The majority of the games can be played alone, or with friends or family. It is, of course, always fun if the grown-ups join in, but just as enjoyable with a friend or favourite toy. If you are busy and your child is playing alone, you could perhaps join in by giving telephone orders for your child to deliver to you and perhaps to toys living at different addresses around the home.

Setting up the game, whether it be a funfair, a fish and chip shop or a farm, is all part of the fun, although some younger children may need a little help. The idea, together with play materials, is usually sufficient to spark the imagination. However, a few questions about who they are and what they are doing or going to do next may help; otherwise some suggestions from you will often help things along if the game appears to be 'running out of steam'.

ANIMAL GAMES

ZOO

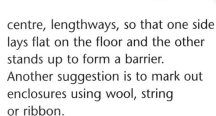

Materials:
- toy animals
- cages: cardboard boxes
- enclosures: boxes, Lego/ wooden bricks, card
- food: pretend, Lego bricks, dry pasta
- keeper: child or play people
- brush: old shaving or tooth brush
- keeper's coat: old shirt, blouse or apron

Cages can be simply made by laying cardboard boxes on one side with the open top facing the front. Twigs or play things can be placed inside the cages with the animals.

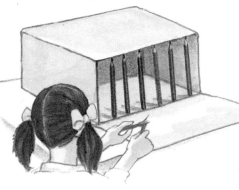

Enclosures can be made by cutting down the height of the sides of a box to form fence-like sides. Fences can be made with Lego bricks or wooden building blocks. Alternatively, strips of card can be folded along the

centre, lengthways, so that one side lays flat on the floor and the other stands up to form a barrier. Another suggestion is to mark out enclosures using wool, string or ribbon.

Your child can be the zoo keeper or manipulate play people. The animals can be swept out, groomed and fed. Toy tractors or lorries could carry the animal feed around the zoo.

Water areas for aquatic animals can be made by colouring the base of a box or sheet of paper blue.

FARM LAYOUTS

Materials:
- plastic farm animals
- crayons
- cereal boxes

This game is based on the same principle as Zoos.

A box building from the Roadways game (page **28**) could be used as a farmhouse.

For those children who enjoy drawing, supply a large sheet of paper (perhaps a length from a roll of lining or computer paper) and a box of crayons. They could draw a farmhouse where the farmer might live, a pond for the ducks and mark out fields for the different animals. Colouring it all will keep them occupied for some time. The animals could then be placed in the drawn enclosures.

VETS

Materials:
- toy animals/cuddly toys
- bandages (see Hospitals)
- large cardboard boxes
- shoe boxes
- white coat: old shirt/blouse

A reception area can be set up with cards in a box for each pet. Older children can write the pet's name on each card. An appointment book can be made. Some chairs or cushions can be put around the waiting area, and the animals can be carried in shoe boxes with holes punched in the lid. Cards can be carried through to the surgery where the vet can inspect the animal, dispense medicine in clear plastic bottles and bandage legs.

PET SHOWS

Materials:
- toy animals/cuddly toys
- trophies and rosettes (see below)
- boxes
- leads: wool/string/belts

Trophies for prizes can be built from Lego bricks. To make rosettes cut 3 circles of paper each of a different diameter, colour with paint or crayon and stick on top of each other with the largest circle at the bottom and smallest on the top. Sticky tape the centre of a length of string or wool to the back of the rosettes to enable them to be tied around the animals' necks.

Rostrums for the top three pets can be made from upturned boxes of different size.

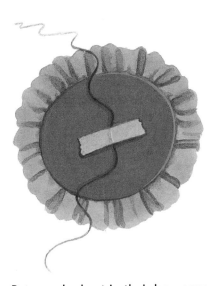

Dolls and play people make a good audience as all the children will want to participate in the show.

Pets can be kept in their box pens while waiting to be shown.
The arena can be a cleared area of floor around which the pets can be carried or walked by tying a lead around the neck and pulling.

It is helpful to suggest that there is a different competition for each type of animal.

CAFÉS AND RESTAURANTS

Materials:
- tablecloths: tea towels, old cot sheets
- plastic tea set/picnic set
- plastic beakers
- plastic box lids for plates
- stainless steel items
- cutlery
- old pans
- apron and tray

The tablecloths can be spread over stools, play tables, coffee tables, upturned cardboard boxes or the floor, with customers seated around. Toys, friends, or family can all be customers.

If a number of children are playing together then perhaps one child could be the cook, another the waiter/waitress and the remainder could be customers. Roles could be swapped at intervals.

If a child is playing on their own, the cafe could be self-service with imaginary customers making their own choice of the food which the cook has prepared earlier. The child playing the game could be the cook, then the waiter/waitress or customer.

WAITER/WAITRESS:
A coffee table or upturned boxes could provide a counter from which to serve. A pad and pencil for taking orders could be provided for older children who may also like to make menus. Preschool children will be quite content to hand over imaginary money but older children may prefer to use play money (see page **24**).

KITCHEN:
Cooking and making the imaginary food is great fun, and for this an upturned box makes a good cooker.

Cooking rings and knobs can be drawn onto the box. An empty washing-up bowl makes an acceptable sink with perhaps a dry dish cloth and tea towel provided. Imaginary food is the least restricting. However, suggestions for play food can be found on page **22**.

TAKE-AWAY ORDERS:
If a telephone is installed on the counter (see Offices) then telephone orders could be taken. The food could be placed in plastic storage boxes or washed foil trays and wrapped in newspaper. They could then be delivered to different addresses around the home.

DRIVE-THRU FAST FOOD:
The seat of an open backed dining chair could be used as a counter. The back of the chair could be used as a window through which wrapped orders (see above) could be passed to drive-thru customers. It would be useful if lots of chips were available for this part of the game (see Fish and Chip Shops, page **30**).

COPS AND ROBBERS

Materials:

Policeman:
- old blue shirt
- belt, hat
- whistle
- Panda car: sit and ride toy
- handcuffs: see below
- walkie talkie: small food packet

Robber:
- swag bag: pillow case
- mask: see below
- bobble hat and scarf

A police station can be made with a counter and an enclosed area to be used as a jail. Under the table makes an ideal jail with the dining/kitchen chairs placed with their backs to the table.

This game is better with more than one child. They can take it in turns to be the policeman or the robber.

Handcuffs can be made by cutting two circles of sturdy card into wide spirals and cutting the centre part of the spiral out. These can be joined together with string or wool.

A simple mask can be made from a cereal packet or paper plate by cutting out a figure eight shape. The centres of the circles should be removed. A length of soft elastic should be attached to the ends of the mask to fit comfortably around the head.

The robber will need goods to 'steal' - perhaps from a shop already set up or jewellery from the dressing-up box.

COWBOYS AND INDIANS

Materials:

Cowboy:
- hat
- gun or shaped twig
- lasso: piece of rope or a spare length of washing line
- chaps: tracksuit trousers or shapes cut out of cardboard

Indian:
- headdress: see below
- tomahawk: wooden spoon
- face paint: see below
- wigwam: any idea from Tents and Dens (page **38**)

An Indian headdress can be made from cutting some feather shapes from cereal boxes and colouring them with bright wax crayons. These can either be attached with a stapler (staples facing out) or taped to a headband or long strip of card which in turn can be attached to a bobble hat to make it comfortable to wear.

Ordinary make-up or face paint sticks can be used, but the following is a tried and tested recipe for face paint:

Mix equal parts of dry, non-toxic powder paint and baby lotion. If it gets too thick, a few drops of water can be added.

The make-up is easy to apply with a sponge or brush. Most colours wash off easily but it is recommended that black and purple be avoided when possible.

Face painting can be used to create witches, clowns, monsters and aliens as well as Indians.

FAIRIES, PRINCES AND PRINCESSES

Materials:

Fairies:
- wand: wooden spoon
- tutu: net curtaining
- headband: see below

Princes:
- cloak: piece of material tied at neck
- crown: party hat or see below

Princesses:
- headwear: see below
- any 'floaty' material tied around waist or shoulders

A star shape cut from a cereal box and covered in foil can be attached to a strip of material or Alice band for a fairy. A similar star can also be attached to the 'spoon' wand with a rubber band or Bluetak.

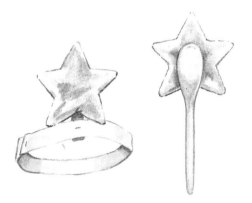

Cut a long strip from a giant cereal box in an even zigzag shape along one edge and join with glue or sticky tape to form a crown. Colour or cover with foil. A headdress can either be a piece of net held in place by an Alice band or a pointed hat made from a newspaper cone with a piece of very lightweight material attached to the top.

A castle to be rescued from, or for Sleeping Beauty to be found in, can be made from cutting square shapes out of the top edge of a cardboard box to give a turreted effect. This can be placed on top of a dining/kitchen table.

FUNFAIRS

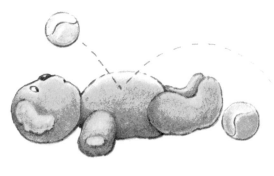

Materials:
- lucky dip: bucket, small toys, newspaper
- roll-a-mat: round table mats or coasters
- skittles: empty plastic bottles, soft ball
- pot shy: empty yoghurt pots, soft ball
- hole-in-one: bucket, bat, soft ball

The Lucky Dip is usually the favourite. Ask your child to collect lots of small toys (cars, rubbers, crayons, combs, hair bobbles etc.) and then supply plenty of old newspaper/magazine pages to wrap them in. These can then be placed in a bucket/empty basket with a cloth over the top.

Roll-a-mat can be made by utilising some round table mats or coasters. The idea is to roll the mat over the line from a given point.

Skittles can be easily set up using empty plastic drinks bottles. Sponge balls are ideal for inside use to avoid any accidents.

A pot shy can be made from a pyramid of upturned empty yoghurt pots on a chair. These can be knocked down by throwing a sponge ball or table tennis ball or a duster tied up into knots.

Hole-in-one is played by batting or throwing a soft ball into a bucket from a given point, which can be quite frustrating but very rewarding when it goes in.

GARAGES

Materials:
- toy cars
- large cardboard box
- petrol pumps: small boxes
- screwdriver: teaspoon handle, biro top

If a garage is required for toy cars, then a large upturned cardboard box with one end cut out will allow cars to be driven into it.

Petrol pumps can be made from blocks of Lego. Alternatively empty spice containers or food drums can be used. A piece of string can be sellotaped to the side for the fuel hose. A small piece of Sellotape wrapped around the other end will make a firm nozzle.

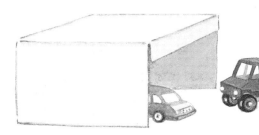

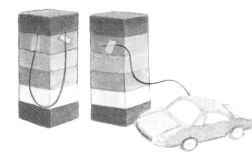

A small ramp can be made out of two parallel low walls of Lego bricks held firmly on a Lego base, on top of which a toy car can be balanced. Repairs can be made to vehicles using pretend tools or improvised tools such as teaspoon handles, Lego bricks, unleaded pencils or biro tops.

A car wash can be made with a piece of card placed in an upturned 'U' shape to form a tunnel through which the cars can be pushed. A dry duster can be used to polish the cars after their wash.

HAIRDRESSERS

Materials:
- basin: empty washing-up bowl
- shampoo/conditioner: empty plastic bottles
- scissors: pretend or plastic
- dryer: pretend, plastic or unplugged dryer
- cape: old scarf, tea towel
- hair spray: toilet roll tube
- brush and comb
- chair or stool
- old towels/face cloths
- mirror

A reception area could be set up with a small table or upturned box with a play telephone or made 'phone (see Offices) and an appointment book/sheets of paper on which to write.

Friends, family or toys can all be customers. Dolls with long hair are ideal.

Clients can be booked in, have their hair washed and towel dried, brushed and combed, cut and blow dried. They can be given magazines to read while they are waiting.

Your child may wish to create a style book to show clients. This can be done by looking through magazines and cutting out different hairstyles for men and women which can be stuck into an exercise book or on loose sheets of paper with water-based glue or Pritt stick.

Many hairdressers sell jewellery and scarves as well as hair products. An assortment of plastic bottles next to the 'till' and a tray of play jewellery will add to this game.

HOSPITALS, DOCTORS, DENTISTS

Materials:
- bandages: material cut into strips (any colour)/ bought bandages
- slings: old scarves
- bedding: old cot sheets/ blankets/towels
- apron: tea towel tucked into waistband
- white coat: old white shirt/blouse
- stethoscope: toy/pretend/old headphones
- crockery: see Cafés and Restaurants
- tray

The settee or cushions on the floor make good beds if friends are patients, although children tend to find this role boring. Toys make more tolerant patients and their beds can be made on the floor, in armchairs or dolls' cots.

HOSPITALS

Bandaging is probably the most enjoyable activity so, if possible, provide lots of strips of material. Gauze bandages are quite cheap to buy, although they do tend to fray with use. Older children could be provided with safety pins to fasten the bandages; younger children can be shown how to tuck the end in or to tie the split end.

If more than one child is playing, one could be the doctor making the patients better and the other the nurse who baths the patients and provides meals. Roles could be swapped.

For reasons of safety, it is best if all medicines are imaginary, although empty plastic bottles which do not resemble medicine bottles and a spoon could be provided.

DOCTORS:

A doctor's surgery is a place your child can relate to, so it may be helpful to allow your child to set up an imaginary surgery similar to that of your local GP. For example, it may include a reception area where patients' names can ticked off in a 'diary'.

A waiting room could be set up in an adjoining room or hallway, or in a separate area of the room. Dining chairs are useful for this. Some magazines or toys could be provided in the waiting room.

The doctor's consulting room could perhaps include the bathroom scales, a play bed, table and chairs, stethoscope and a pad on which the 'doctor' could write prescriptions.

DENTIST:

Reception and waiting room as above.

The dentist's consulting room could perhaps include an old toothbrush if toys are the patients. The dentist could show the patient how to clean their teeth properly.

Many dentists give away badges and these could be made from sticky labels on which your child has drawn a smiley face.

The dentist also needs a bright light to see inside patients' mouths. A small torch, with or without batteries, would be perfect.

LIBRARIES

If possible, allow your child to spread the books, magazines, comics and cassettes around the room on tables, settees, chairs. Older children could perhaps categorise the books etc.

Pieces of card can be placed inside the cover of each book as part of the game. These can be stamped or marked by older children and may be collected when the book is borrowed.

Library tickets can be made from card by utilising old cereal boxes. Tickets and book cards can be placed in a box when the book is out on loan. These can be replaced when the books are returned.

The librarian could direct borrowers to different sections and help them to choose books.

Many activities are held in libraries such as 'Story Time'. The librarian could read a story (if older) or tell a story (if younger). A drawing or colouring competition could be organised.

Many libraries supply photocopying services. A photocopier can be made with an upturned cardboard box and a separate piece of card placed on top to form a lid. Dials and buttons can be drawn on the box.

MAKING MUSIC

Musical instruments, once made, will have quite a long life. They can be used for shows, pretending to be part of a pop group or accompanying the radio.

SHAKERS
Dried peas, beans, pasta, rice, sand or beads can be placed in plastic bottles with tight screw caps, cardboard boxes, tubes or balloons.

DRUMS
Upturned buckets, bowls or a tin can, covered with thick polythene stretched tight across it. Metal, wooden or plastic spoons can be used as drum sticks.

CLAPPERS
Two pieces of thick dowelling, two flat pieces of sanded wood or two pan lids.

SCRAPERS
Any object with a textured surface such as a cake cooling tray or grill pan rack played by running a wooden, metal or plastic spoon over the surface.

XYLOPHONE
Eight empty bottles of the same size and shape each filled with a different level of water to create different notes. The bottle with the most water will create the lowest note. Using a metal fork, hit each bottle gently.

GUITAR
Strong elastic bands stretched across the middle of an open rigid plastic box. Bands of different thicknesses will create different notes.

ODDMENTS
Bicycle bell. Squeaky toy. Whistle. Anything that makes a good sound.

MUMMIES/ DADDIES

Materials:
- baby bath/sink: washing-up bowl
- cooker: upturned box with controls drawn on
- baby: doll or soft toy
- feeding bottle: empty plastic vinegar bottle/ toy feeding bottle/ empty salt shaker
- cot: doll's pram, box or chair
- bed for mummy/daddy

Housework can also be part of the game. A clean duster and either a dustpan and brush or vacuum cleaner extension make useful play materials.

Create a space for a home, or see Tents and Dens (page 38) for further ideas.

The main purpose of the game is to look after the baby and mimic the adults in the home. The baby can be bottle fed or spoon fed from pretend meals prepared by the child. Baby can be placed in a doll's pram or child's buggy to be taken to the shops. A shopping basket makes a good carrycot. Baby can be bathed and changed before putting to bed.

Washing the baby clothes, either pretend or real, can also be part of the daily routine (see Washing Day, page **47**). An upturned cardboard box with a circle cut out of one side makes a good automatic washing machine.

OFFICES

Materials:
- pens, pencils and crayons
- paper
- junk mail and blank forms
- used envelopes
- used stamps
- telephone: pretend, plastic or made
- calculator: real, pretend or made
- in tray: plastic box or made

The majority of time tends to be spent filling in paper, forms or writing letters. A few squiggles will suffice for those children who cannot yet write properly. Posting letters and receiving them is fun, as is making lots of telephone calls.

If two children are playing the game, a paper cup at either end of a piece of string will work quite well as an internal telephone. Alternatively, a small flat box such as an empty chocolate box can be covered in

paper on which telephone buttons can be drawn. A flat strip of card to lay on the top will act as a receiver. Calculators can be made in a similar way.

In trays can quickly be made by taping the ends of a cereal box and cutting out the front to form a tray.

Empty margarine tubs can be used for stamps, rubbers, rubber bands and other small office items. Beakers can be used as pencil tidies.

For photocopier, see Libraries (page **18**).

For post box, see Post Offices (page **25**).

PLAY FOOD

A variety of play food adds to the enjoyment of several of the games included in this book. Although play food can be purchased from toy shops, a wider range can be improvised or made at home.

Listed below are just some of the ideas which have been used successfully.

From around the home:
- bath sponge
- cakes
- beads and marbles (ages 5+)
- card bread slices
- dried pulses
- empty tubs, cartons, sachets, plastic bottles, food packets
- jigsaw pieces
- Lego bricks
- paper plate pizzas
- pasta shapes
- pebbles
- pegs for chips
- scrunched paper potato balls
- washed vegetables

FORMELLO FOOD

This is a plasticine-type product which can be found in most art and model shops. It is available in a wide range of colours. The items, once modelled, must be baked but do not require painting or varnishing. Once opened, it keeps well in an air-tight container.

However, a less expensive alternative would be to use the dough food ideas on the next page.

PLAY DOUGH FOOD

These items, once made, are very hard-wearing and will last indefinitely.

Make up the dough recipe found on page **24**. Model into the required food items, ideas for which are listed below. Dough about ¹/₂″ thick will take about 30 minutes to bake at 160°C/325°F/Gas Mark 3. Allow longer for thicker items. Once the items are cold paint, if wished, with poster paint which must be allowed to dry before coating with a non-toxic varnish.

Bread rolls Make a ball of dough and slightly flatten.

Chops Shape dough. Paint a red comma shape leaving a broad border along the outside curved edge.

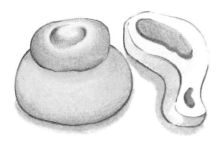

Cottage loaves As for bread rolls, but add a slightly smaller second layer.

Jam sandwiches Make triangle shapes and paint a thin line of red in the centre of the edges.

Jam tarts Roll and cut out pastry in the usual way. Bake in shallow bun trays. Paint red in centre.

Oranges Make a ball with the dough. Use a fork to give a dimpled effect. Colour orange.

Potatoes Mould into irregular shapes. Colour brown.

Sponge slices As for jam sandwiches, but make the triangle deeper.

Other ideas Apples, bananas, carrots, fish, tomatoes.

Play food made on a reduced scale is easy to handle and is equally effective. It also has the advantage of being more cost effective.

PLAY MONEY

It is a good idea to make a large stock of money as some will inevitably get lost or torn.

COINS

Circles of cardboard from cereal packets work best. The coins may need to be slightly larger than life size for little hands to cope with. Coin values written in black marker pen are useful for children learning to recognise numbers and count.

Appropriate colouring assists recognition:

Old buttons or beads make suitable coins for school-aged children.

NOTES

Thin card works better than paper as it is more durable, but paper is more realistic. Try rectangles of newspaper or notepaper. Notepaper can be coloured and the values written on if it would be suitable for your child.

PLAY DOUGH RECIPE

2 cups plain flour

1 cup salt

1 cup water

1 tsp. oil

Mix the above ingredients together. The addition of salt preserves the dough which can be stored in an airtight container in the fridge for further use. Add food colouring to make the dough more interesting. Dough that has become too dry can be restored by placing in a food mixer to reduce to 'crumbs' and adding a little water. If the dough seems too wet, add more flour until the consistency feels right.

POST OFFICES

Materials:
- stamps cut from incoming mail
- old junk mail to deliver
- unrequired forms
- old envelopes and postcards
- cheap ink pads/rubber stamps
  (from toy shops/stationers)
- pencils
- licences (see below)
- post box
- toy or pretend telephone
  (see Offices)
- play money
- margarine tubs

A few ideas are listed above for constantly renewable resources for your child's Post Office.

Stocks of licences (e.g. Dog, TV, Car) can easily be made by cutting up paper into regular sizes. Draw a few lines on which the child can write, leaving room for an 'official' stamp.

You may be able to obtain old computer print-outs or rolls of lining paper can be bought cheaply from a wallpaper shop. Margarine tubs are useful for keeping rubber bands, paperclips, stamps and licences tidy.

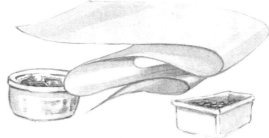

A post box can be made by cutting a slit in the side of a large washing powder or cardboard box which can be painted or coloured red. Junk mail can be posted and collected.

Quite a lot is needed to make an interesting selection to be delivered by the postman. A shoulder bag is useful for deliveries.

PUPPET SHOWS

Hand puppets are easily manipulated and are very good for stimulating imagination and helping to develop vocabulary. Younger children like to act out nursery rhymes and children's stories whilst some older children prefer to create original puppet shows.

It is not necessary to set up a puppet theatre. The back of a settee or arm chair makes a useful stage providing cover for the puppeteers.

A table covered with a floor length cloth is equally effective.

A large variety of puppets is not required, either. An effective show can be achieved with two simple sock puppets and lots of imagination.

PAPER PLATE PUPPETS

Two paper plates per puppet are required. Draw a face on the back of one plate and hair on the back of the other. Tape or staple the rims of the plates together leaving a gap at the neck large enough for the child's hand.

PAPER BAG PUPPETS

Draw a face on a paper bag or used large envelope with the open end at the bottom. Screw the top corners to form ears. Place the bag over the hand. Gather the open edge around the wrist and tuck into a cuff.

STICK PUPPETS

Almost any head can be fixed to either a small piece of dowelling or short length of garden cane. Heads can be made from stuffed socks, paper plates, strong paper bags filled with screwed-up newspaper or old tennis or table tennis balls. Features can be drawn with marker pens.

SIMPLE SOCK PUPPETS

The child's hand is placed in the foot of the sock with the fingers placed in the toe part and the thumb in the heel. The sole part of the sock is pushed in to form the mouth.

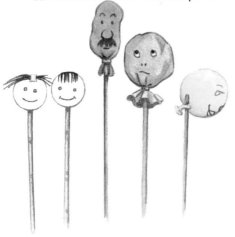

Gather a piece of material around the neck of the puppet and hold in place with an elastic band.
Large handkerchiefs, dusters, scarves or tea towels are suitable.
Costumes can also be dolls' clothes or very small baby garments.

The gummed edge of an unused envelope will make up to four pairs of eyes which can be stuck in position. Sewn on buttons can also be used.

Effective stick puppets can also be made from cheap wooden spoons.

ROADWAYS AND VILLAGES

Materials:
- small ball of wool in a colour contrasting to the carpet
- toy cars
- empty boxes and cereal packets (different sizes)

Road and town layouts can utilise as much or as little of the floor space as you are prepared to have taken up.

Lengths of wool marking out roadways and car parks are easy for children to use. Wool is easily manipulated to make bendy roads but will only stay in place on a piled carpeted surface. Your child may need some help initially, but will soon be able to create exciting layouts.

with a few crayons or a dab of paint, although they can be bulky to store. If garages are made, one end of the box can be left open to enable the cars to be driven in. Building blocks, Lego and Stickle bricks can also be used to good effect.

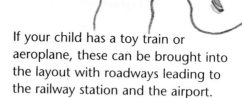

If your child has a toy train or aeroplane, these can be brought into the layout with roadways leading to the railway station and the airport.

Jar lids or cream cheese boxes make good roundabouts. Empty cereal and food boxes make good buildings and can quite easily be transformed into a house, shop, hospital or garage

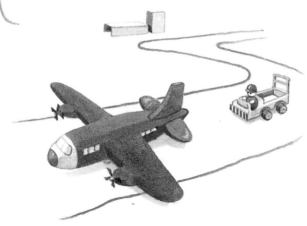

SCHOOLS

Materials:
- blackboard and easel: bought or made
- tables: coffee table, upturned sturdy box
- chairs: stools, cushions
- chalk and cloth or damp sponge for cleaning
- paper, pencils, rubbers, rulers, crayons
- reading books
- bell or rattle
- apron/old shirt for messy activities

An easel is not necessary. A home-made board can be placed on the seat of a dining chair propped up against the back. It may be advisable to put a cloth over the seat of the chair to avoid chalk dust.

Blackboards can easily be made. Use a suitably sized piece of hardboard and sandpaper the edges to make smooth. Tins of blackboard paint can be bought at hardware stores and are inexpensive.

Paint several coats onto the smooth side of the hardboard. Chalk can also be used directly onto the side of a cardboard box.

The teacher should have a desk and chair. A bell is useful to ring at the end of lessons.

Suggested activities could include: reading, drawing, colouring, painting, cutting out and sticking, jigsaws, modelling from plasticine or play dough (see page **24**), playtime, registration.

SHOPS

Central to each shop is a counter which can be made from a kitchen/coffee table or upturned sturdy cardboard boxes.

Younger children may want to use pretend money whilst school-aged children may prefer to use play money (see page **24**).

Plastic boxes or empty margarine tubs keep play money tidy. Magazines and old newspapers are a cheap source of wrapping paper and used large envelopes make handy paper bags. These can also be made by rolling newspaper into a cone and screwing the paper at the bottom. Older children may wish to make price tickets out of card.

FISH AND CHIP SHOP

Materials:
- fish: cut from cardboard
- chips: a pile of pegs
- sausages: brown toilet roll tubes
- pies: clean empty foil pie dishes
- peas/gravy: clean empty yoghurt pots plus pans and ladles
- fryer: cardboard or plastic boxes
- vinegar: empty plastic bottle or pretend
- salt: empty salt cruet or pretend
- wrapping: old newspapers
- scoop: small plastic seaside spade

Your child may need to be shown how to wrap the fish and chips and school-aged children may prefer to use dried peas rather than pretend. Once again, telephone orders of different quantities can be taken and delivered.

CLOTHES SHOP

Materials:
- any unwanted clothes (including night clothes)
- jewellery
- shoes, hats, bags, gloves, scarves
- net curtains (for brides)
- old curtains (for cloaks)
- ribbons, lace, belts

Unwanted items of clothing from family and friends can be gathered together to form a dressing-up box, the contents of which can be used to play Clothes Shops. These items can also be used to enhance other games.

GROCERY SHOP AND SUPER-MARKET

Materials:
- contents of your kitchen cupboards (*except* cleaning products, toiletries and medicines)
- empty washed yoghurt pots, ice-cream cartons etc.
- pasta shapes and dried pulses to weigh (4 years+)
- washed vegetables
- play food
- scales

Goods should be displayed in the shop. Encourage your child to put similar items together. Loose food can be stored in plastic boxes which the shop assistant will need to weigh and place in paper bags. Telephone orders can be taken, packed in boxes and delivered to addresses around the home.

Kitchen units or settees and chairs make good supermarket shelves. A doll's pram or toy wheelbarrow can be used as a supermarket trolley. The cash desk can be placed near the door.

NEWSAGENT

SHOE SHOP

Materials:
- old newspapers, magazines and comics
- old sweet wrappers re-wrapped around a ball of tissue paper
- empty chocolate boxes and sweet tubes
- sweet bar wrappers sellotaped around cardboard
- pencils
- crayons
- colouring books
- old Christmas/birthday cards and postcards
- small toys

Materials:
- men's, women's and children's shoes
- shoes from the dressing-up box
- slippers
- boots
- socks
- bags

It is a good idea to display just one of each pair and put the other in the stock room which could be behind the settee or in the next room. Finding the matching pair is part of the game.

Newspapers printed on modern presses do not leave hands inky black any more, so they are a good play material.

Delivering newspapers can be included in this game. Newspapers, magazines and comics could be delivered to different addresses around the home using a shopping bag or basket.

This is a good opportunity to introduce the skills of tying laces and fastening buckles.

The shopkeeper could help customers to choose cards and presents.

SPACESHIPS

Materials:
- spaceship: see Tents and Dens
- space-suit: pretend or from dressing up box
- boots: Wellington boots
- helmet: small cardboard box
- oxygen tanks: 2 litre clear plastic drink bottles
- control panel: upturned box
- moon buggy: sit and ride toy
- walkie-talkies: small empty food packet
- bucket and spade

A control panel for the spaceship can be made from an upturned box on which lots of dials have been drawn.

Space walks can be made to repair the rocket or satellites. Space equipment can be made from foil covered cardboard tubes protruding at different angles from a large carton or box.

If a space-suit is required, some suggestions have been listed above. Loops of string can be taped to the plastic bottles enabling them to be slung over the shoulders. A helmet can be made by cutting a square out the front of a small, light cardboard box, which can be placed over the head to sit on the shoulders.

A bucket and spade can be taken on buggy expeditions to collect moon rocks made from scrunched-up balls of paper.

However, an imaginary space-suit can be as elaborate as wished!

SPORTS DAY

This outdoor game, based on school sports days, is best played on grass to avoid possible injury. A starter/organiser is needed but prizes are not necessary.

WATER RACE

Materials:
- buckets/bowls containing water
- plastic beakers of equal size
- bowls and measuring jug

A container of water is placed at the end of each lane with empty containers on the starting line. Each child is given a beaker with which to transfer water from one end to the other in the quickest time over 3 or 5 laps.

The child with the most water in the quickest time wins. The water from each container can be measured in a jug.

OBSTACLE RACE

Materials:
- jump: brush balanced on buckets/bricks
- crawl: under picnic table/row of chairs
- balance: along a plank of wood
- throw: a ball into bucket from given place

If possible, set up two of everything, otherwise the first to get to the obstacle gets the advantage. Allow one ball for each child.

THREE-LEGGED RACE

Materials:
- scarves, ties or strips of cloth

Two children stand side by side. The middle two legs are tied together to form 'one' leg. The first couple to the finish line is the winner.

DRESSING UP RACE

Materials:
- scarves, hats, gloves, old skirts, coats etc.

Place similar items of clothing at intervals along each lane.
The children must run to each item and put them on in turn. The first one to return to the starting line is the winner.

EGG AND SPOON RACE

Materials:
- soft balls and seaside spades
- hard-boiled eggs and large spoons

Run or walk quickly with the egg balanced on the spoon. If the egg is dropped, the child should stop and pick up the egg and restart from where it was dropped.

SKIPPING RACE

Materials:
- skipping ropes

Friends can usually provide some extra skipping ropes. Children skip whilst running.

POTATO RACE

Materials:
- seaside/household buckets/ plastic bowls/boxes
- potatoes

Potatoes are placed at intervals along each running lane. The children leave the bucket on the starting line, collect the nearest potato, run back to the start and place it in the bucket. They then collect each potato in turn. The first child to return to the starting line having placed all the potatoes in the bucket is the winner.

SWIMMING POOLS

Materials:
- dolls or plastic play figures
- coloured rubber bands
- paddling pool/baby bath
- tickets: card or pegs
- lockers: small boxes tipped on the side
- towels: old face cloths, tea towels, towels

This game is not suitable for small children who need to be very closely supervised with shallow water. Suggested age is 5 and upwards. It is suitable for playing outdoors with an adult supervisor.

A paddling pool or baby bath should be partially filled with water. Dolls or play figures can attend the swimming pool.

The doll's clothes can be stored in lockers made from empty cereal packets laid flat with the opening end accessible to open and close.

The visitors can be placed in the water and 'swim' around, or your child could be a swimming instructor and give lessons.

Swimmers wearing the same coloured bands come out of the pool at the same time. They then need to be dried and dressed.

Tickets can be sold and coloured rubber bands issued which can be put on the doll's arm or leg.

TEA PARTIES AND PICNICS

Materials:
- old tablecloth/blanket/towel
- play tea-set or plastic beakers, plastic box lids, etc.
- drink: pretend or water/ lemonade (non-staining)
- food: pretend, play food or real

Picnics and tea parties can be held inside or out. It is not necessary to have other children present as imaginary friends or toys can be the guests.

Other ideas for small amounts of picnic food include segments of fruit, sultanas, a few crisps or a couple of biscuits.

Washing up at the kitchen sink afterwards can be a part of the game.

Pretend food is less restricting, but play food (see page **22**) or a small amount of real food is more satisfying. This can be as simple as water to pour from the teapot and a slice of bread and butter.

Picnic style meals could be served at lunchtimes and incorporated into other games, e.g. refreshments on an aircraft, in a den, on a spaceship or food in a café or restaurant.

TENTS AND DENS

Materials:
- frame: clotheshorse, airer, washing line, table
- cover: blanket or sheet
- ground: old carpet, rug, blanket or towel
- crockery: plastic play tea-set or plastic beakers, bowls, boxes, lids, imaginary
- bed: cushions and old blankets or towels

Tents or dens can be made anywhere, inside or out. The quickest tent to make is a blanket or bedspread thrown over a kitchen or dining table.
If a clothes' horse/airer is used, the ground edges need to be wedged to prevent possible collapse.

An outside washing line can be allowed to sag with a blanket thrown over and the ground edges weighted down. Pegs are excellent for closing the ends. A collapsed lilo makes a good groundsheet if the tent is outside and the ground slightly damp.

The space behind a settee pulled away from the wall can often be utilised with a sheet wedged behind the cushions and, say, a radiator.

If there is more than one child and you have the equipment, it is sometimes fun for each child to have their own tent.

TOP OF THE POPS

Materials:
- tape of pop songs or favourite songs
- tape recorder
- dressing up box
- microphone: spoon, cardboard tube
- stage: cleared area of floor, rug

This is a game for older children to play with brothers, sisters or friends. A considerable amount of time can be spent working out dance routines and costumes and practising miming to the music. Quite often they may wish to do this in private, perhaps in a bedroom, so that you, the audience, do not see the performances before the production.

One child not in a particular routine can introduce the act and start and stop the music. This can be taken in turns.

If the show is to be performed outside, sheets can be thrown over a washing line to form curtains for the stage.

They may wish to make invitations which they can give out and collect in 'at the door'. They may also wish to provide simple refreshments of drinks and biscuits to the audience during the interval. This game relies on a live audience, so be prepared to watch and to have some of their friends round for the performance.

TRANSPORT

AIRPORTS

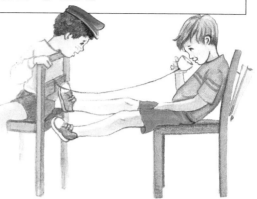

Materials:
- seats: chairs, cushions, upturned boxes
- tickets: rectangular pieces of card
- money: pretend or play money (page **24**)
- trolley: doll's pram, wash basket, cardboard box, play trolley
- counter: table, upturned box
- luggage: old handbags, shopping bags

SHOPS

It is usual for travellers to purchase sweets and magazines for the journey and a small shop could be set up on a coffee table, chair or upturned box (see Newsagents, page **32**).

CHECK-IN

This could consist of a counter where tickets are sold and paid for with either pretend or play money. Older children could write the destination on the tickets or they could be left blank. Luggage could be stored behind the desk and later taken onto the aeroplane.

AEROPLANE

The aeroplane could be placed at the far end of the room or in an adjoining room so that passengers have to walk to it. Tickets can be collected as passengers alight. The interior of the plane could consist of chairs or cushions placed in rows with an aisle between. A pilot's seat could be placed at the front.

The steward(ess) could serve refreshments from a trolley pulled down the centre. If your child is playing alone with toys, the roles can be played in turn.

ROWING BOAT

Cushions on the floor, an airbed/lilo, settee or a large cardboard box are some suggestions which could form a rowing boat. Paddles or oars can be strips of card, large spoons, seaside spades or pretend.

Rowing boats can be used to row down the river for a picnic or out to an island. Deciding on the destination, rowing, jumping ashore and tying up the boat are all part of the game.

The rowing boats could be hired out. Tickets can be made from card and pretend or play money could be used.

CAR FERRY

The ferry could go across a river or across the sea. Toy or pretend cars could be driven on with tickets sold and change given.

Cars could be directed to their correct place on the ferry. The ferry needs to be untied at the beginning and moored at the end of the journey. Passengers could have cabins with beds and a café or restaurant could be on the ferry (see page **8**). The captain could steer the ship and give the orders.

CONTAINER SHIP

A bed, settee or space marked out on the floor with cushions could form the ship. Cardboard boxes could be used as containers and your child could decide what the containers hold. These would need to be loaded and stored on the ship and paperwork could be given to the captain. The destination would have to be decided. The ship's crew could have cabins.

A large cardboard box could be used as the ship, which could be pulled round the home by attached string. It could be loaded in one room and offloaded in another.

PIRATE SHIP

A good game to play with others. Old headscarves tied around the head, rolled up trouser legs and bare feet are sufficient to give atmosphere to the game. Toilet roll or kitchen paper tubes make good telescopes with which to spy other ships.

Cardboard boxes for treasure will suffice. Play jewellery or play money could also be used for treasure.

The pirates could take the treasure back to an island and hide it. Captain Hook in Peter Pan is a pirate with which children can identify.

BUSES

Materials:
- tickets: pieces of card, pegs
- money: play money
- seats: chairs, cushions
- bell: bell, rattle, pretend
- plastic boxes

The seating could be formed by rows of chairs or cushions with an aisle down the middle. Alternatively, if playing with a few friends or toys, they could all climb on the bed or the settee with the driver sitting at one end.

A narrow upturned box could be placed next to the driver's seat on top of which could be placed plastic boxes containing tickets and play money.

Passengers could shout or ring a bell to stop the bus when they want to get off.

Routes and destinations could be decided by the driver.

Alternatively a cardboard box could be pulled around the home by string, stopping at different bus stops (see Trains).

If chairs are used, the driver could have a chair at the front of the bus and a dashboard could be made by drawing controls on an upturned cardboard box.

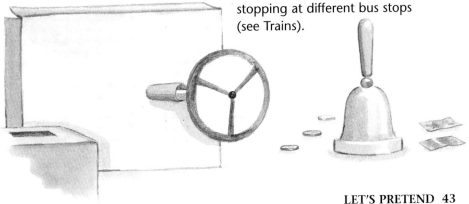

FIRE ENGINES

Materials:
- uniform: raincoat
- wellington boots
- hat
- hose: vacuum cleaner extension,
  unconnected hose pipe,
  pretend
- toy animals

The fire engine can be static if played indoors - a bed, the settee or just a chair for the driver. The vacuum cleaner extension makes a suitably clean fire hose for indoor play which can be rolled up and placed on the engine.

Fires can be in different rooms or different parts of the garden. One room or part of a room could be set aside as the fire station where the engine could be 'cleaned' after each fire. An empty bucket and dry cloth could be useful play items.

A loop of string attached to a large cardboard box will allow your child to pull the part of the engine which stores the hose around the home or outside. An imaginary engine is the most mobile. The voice is the best siren, but if a bell is available this could also be used.

Firemen are also asked to rescue animals from difficult, hard to reach places. Toy animals could be placed around the room, ready to be rescued.

RACING CARS

Materials:
- toy cars
- cardboard/cereal packets
- Lego bricks/
  wooden building blocks

A circuit can be marked out with strips of card from old cereal boxes which have been folded along the middle, lengthways, so that one half lays flat on the floor and the other half stands up to form a barrier.

This is a game which can be played either alone or with a friend.
Toy cars can be used or cars made from Lego. Toy or pretend fire engines, tow trucks or ambulances can be utilised when the cars crash.

Alternatively, lengths of wool will 'stick' to a piled carpet and curve easily. Lego bricks or wooden blocks can mark out the track or be built to form crash barriers on the bends.
A piece of card or wool laid across the track can form the starting line.

A small cardboard box with the flap open at one end can be placed in the central reservation and used as a pit stop for changing tyres and refuelling (see Garages on page **14**).

TRAINS

Materials:
- tickets: pieces of card, pegs
- money: play money
- carriages: cardboard boxes, wash basket
- seats: chairs, cushions
- whistle: whistle, voice

Seating, if used, should be placed in rows with an aisle down the middle to enable the guard to sell or check tickets. An old handbag with a shoulder strap is useful for keeping money and tickets in.

Your child could be the driver pulling the train around the room or the home to different stations. Different passengers could get on and off the train.

The guard could blow a whistle, ring a bell or shout to tell the driver it is safe to leave the station.

A driver's chair could be placed at the front of the train and a dashboard could be made from an upturned cardboard box with controls drawn on.

Another idea is to string cardboard boxes (with sharp staples removed) together to form a train in which toys could be placed as passengers.

For a change, the train could be used to carry goods - toys, small packets and play bricks which can be loaded in one room and offloaded in another.

WASHING DAY

Materials:
- washing-up bowl or baby bath
- warm water
- low level washing line
- pegs
- detergent: washing-up liquid (for bubbles)
- clothes: dolls' clothes or small items
  e.g. socks, tea towels, hankies

A generous squirt of washing-up liquid in a sink half full of warm water will provide sufficient bubbles to last the wash.

If this activity takes place in the kitchen, it is a good idea to let your child use the sink to wash in and have the washing-up bowl on the draining board in which to put all the dripping clothes.

A nail brush could be provided for scrubbing. A quick final spin in the washing machine, if convenient, is usually a good idea to prevent the washing dripping and taking a long time to dry. The bowl can then be used as an appropriate sized washing basket to carry the washing outside.

A low level washing line can be strung around a swing frame, between bushes, trees and fences or between the backs of two chairs.

Pegging out the clothes is an essential part of the game.
Clothes can be pegged to an airer.

WITCHES, WIZARDS AND GHOSTS

Materials:
- witch's cauldron: washing up bowl
- wizard's cloak: any large piece of material
- pointed hat: see below
- broomstick: brush or feather duster
- cat: cuddly toy
- spell book
- ghosts: any white material (old sheet)

A fire for the cauldron can be made from scrunching up some red tissue or crepe paper with a few twigs, or using the twigs on their own.

The witch's brew for the cauldron can be made from shredded newspaper.

The easiest way to decorate the hat is to draw suns, moons and stars onto newspaper with a marker pen before the paper is folded into a cone and Sellotaped.

Face painting can be used for the wizard (see page 11).

A ghost outfit should be white if possible. A small sheet or towel can be tied round the shoulders and an old pillowcase can go over the head with slits cut out for eyes and mouth. If an old pillowcase is not available, a mask can be made from card.
To make the outfit really gruesome, red food dye can be dropped down the front to look like blood.